KYOTO GARDENS

by Kinsaku Nakane

translated by
    Money L. Hickman
        &
    Kaichi Minobe

 HOIKUSHA

CONTENTS

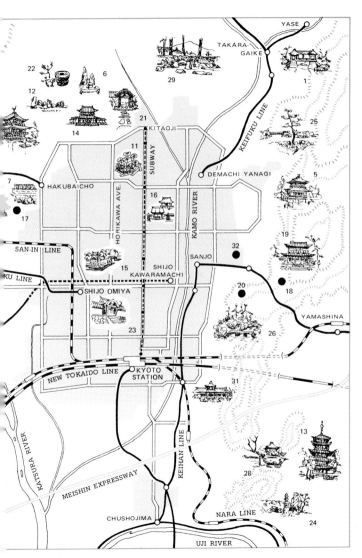

Cover Photo: Ryôan-ji

KYOTO GARDENS

by Kinsaku Nakane

translated by M.L.Hickman & Kaichi Minobe

© All rights reserved. No.9 of Hoikusha's Color Books Series. Published by Hoikusha Publishing Co., Ltd., 17-13, 1-chome, Uemachi, Higashi-ku, Osaka, 540 Japan. ISBN 4-586-54009-5. First Edition in 1965. Revised in 1977. Twenty-first Edition in 1985. Printed in JAPAN

Shugakuin Rikyû (Shugakuin Imperial Villa)

From the Rin-un-tei, the structure at its highest point, an excellent panorama of the Kyoto countryside greets the visitor's eye.

Saihô-ji

The moss garden looks bright and beautiful as the sun's rays slant across trees. In old times, there were a waterfall and several houses around the pond.

3

Saihô-ji

Before the temple was razed in the Ônin Wars, many buildings stood on this site. Central structure in the complex was the Shari-den ("Reliquary Hall"), a splendid two-storied building. The lower story of this structure was **known as the Ruri-den ("Lapis Lazuli Hall"), while the** second story contained a Buddha relic, enshrined in a miniature crystal pagoda. The Shari-den stood on the western side of the pond, a position of central importance in reference to the layout of the garden. Similar concepts were followed by the Ashikaga Shogun Yoshimitsu, who had his Kinkaku pavilion (which was also a Shari-den, with an enshrined relic) built facing a pond; and by Yoshimasa,

The stone arrangement for the stone steps to the hill top

The upper pond of the "Moss Temple"

who had part of his Ginkaku pavilion designed after the prototype of the Ruri-den, and oriented toward the east, looking out over a similar body of water. Thus, the Kinkaku and Ginkaku structures were both built with the idea in mind of repeating certain aspects of the architecture and compositional plan of the Saihô-ji Shari-den, and the three buildings must have been similar in their atmosphere of luxurious, refined monasticism. In shape and deployment, the pond was designed to focus attention on the Shari-den, and to present a scene reminiscent of the Buddhist idea of paradise, in which lovely pavilions float above water vistas filled with lotus blossoms.

Tenryû-ji

Compositional focus is centered on the high waterfall in the background and the angular, dynamic stone formations which seem to stand on the surface of the water.

◀ The view from the waterfall. The stone bridge and scattered stones seem to be floating on the pond.

▼ Stone arrangement adjacent to the waterfall

Tenryû-ji

The Tenryû-ji temple was founded in 1339 by Takauji, first of the Ashikaga Shoguns, in memory of the Emperor Daigo, and the distinguished Zen priest Soseki (also known as Musô Kokushi) served as its first abbot. The splendid temple complex, laid out on the site of the former Kameyama Palace, was completed in 1343 and included an extensive garden designed by Soseki, laid out around a pond in front of the abbot's quarters. Fires have repeatedly leveled the temple buildings, but the lovely pond and the essential features of its surrounding garden, such as the

waterfall and various of the rock formations, have survived, essentially intact, to the present day, and still retain the superb character of the original landscape planned by Soseki. Ingeniously designed, the garden is arranged so that it may be seen to best advantage from a variety of vantage points located around its perimeter, as well as from the buildings which face it. Among its noteable features is the compositional scheme and disposition of the great angular rocks, which give the garden its particular atmosphere of crisp beauty.

Rokuon-ji ("Kinkaku-ji")

Designed to evoke an image of the 'seven-treasure pond'
in Buddhist Paradise scenes, this pond originally was filled
with blossoming lotus plants. Although it came to be

known later as the Kinkaku ("Golden Pavilion") in common parlance, the structure was called the Shari-den ("Reliquary Hall") during Yoshimitsu's time. The present building is a faithful reproduction of the original, burned down in a tragic fire in 1950.

Rokuon-ji (Kinkaku-ji, "Golden Pavilion")

Yoshimitsu (1358–1408), third Shogun of the Ashi-kaga period, appropriated a villa site at Kitayama which had belonged to the Saionji Family, and in 1397 he began construction on a series of splendid buildings at the location. Little remains today to give us any idea of the disposition or architecture of the Kitayama Palace, although it is clear that it cost a staggering sum. The names of those responsible for planning and constructing the palace are not known, nor are the locations of the buildings or the layout of the garden, but it is clear that the complex was a fairly extensive one. An entry in a document mentions that the usual ceremony commemorating the erection of pillars and roof timbers was held on April 16th, 1397, and includes the names of a number of the main buildings, as well as a brief comment on the garden. Among these, the Shari-den ("Reliquary Hall"), or Kinkaku ("Golden Pavilion") was the most important structure. A three-storied building of graceful proportions and modest size, it was designed to form an integral unit in combination with the sur-rounding garden. An extensive area was excavated, and a broad lotus-filled pond, large enough for leisurely parties afloat, com-pleted in front of the Kinkaku. Seen from the far side of

The Ryūmon water fall on the slope in the north of the Golden Pavilion

Crane and tortoise islands, from the first story of Kinkaku (Golden Pavilion)

the pond, the gilded structure, set against the dark green mass of Mt. Kinugasa and floating above a sea of lotus blossoms, must certainly have evoked a feeling that the observer was truly present in some sublime Buddhist paradise. Yoshimitsu spent his last years in this splendid monastic retreat, which was converted to a Zen Temple after his death and renamed the Rokuon-ji after the Shogun's posthumous name Rokuon-in. The majority of the buildings in the complex were subsequently moved, or burned down during the Ônin Wars, although the Kinkaku survived until 1950, when it was destroyed by fire. The main aspects of the pond and its adjacent garden seem to have survived without any important changes, in spite of various modifications carried out over the years.

13

Jishô-ji ("Ginkaku-ji")

The superbly designed garden as seen from the Tôgû-dô devotional hall, with the 'white crane' island in the center and the waterfall to the rear left.

High hedges flanking the approachway to the Jishô-ji

Jishô-ji (Ginkaku-ji, "Silver Pavilion")

The Kannon-den ("Hall of the Bodhisattva Kannon", commonly known as the "Ginkaku") and the neighboring Tôgû-dô devotional hall are the sole architectural remains of the palatial villa built by the eighth Ashikaga Shogun, Yoshimasa (1435–90), at the foot of Higashiyama, a low chain of mountains east of Kyoto. Yoshimasa gathered a coterie of outstanding artists, poets and playwrights here, and these men did much to shape the aesthetic taste of the times. Yoshimasa was a knowledgeable patron, and his encouragement of the masters of the Noh drama and Tea Ceremony resulted in significant developments in those arts. Furthermore, his patronage inspired new movements in painting and architecture, as well as a general advance in the level of contemporary artistic awareness.

A great admirer of gardens, he spent much of his time traveling from one famous example to another, and he was particularly fond of the Saihô-ji, which he enjoyed visiting even during a heavy rain. Construction on the Higashiyama villa was begun in 1482 and completed in 1493, three years after his death. Yoshimasa devoted considerable of his time and attention to the layout of the garden, and he had many trees, shrubs and rocks brought from locations distant from Kyoto. Even the desperate Ônin Wars failed to dampen Yoshimasa's addiction for the Saihô-ji, where he sojourned during periods of battle. Consequently, it is not surprising that the influence of its garden is to be seen at the Ginkaku. The noted designer Zeami is said to have worked under Yoshimasa in laying out the garden. The temple was renamed the Jishô-ji following the Shogun's death.

The tranquil atmosphere of Yoshimasa's "Silver Pavilion"

Daisen-in

Two views of the 'dry landscape' garden. Planned as an integral unit and completed in the same year, the garden and shoin structure form an impressive harmony of space, texture, and disposition. The photographs show portions

of one section of the garden which covers only sixty-six square meters. In spite of this small size there is no sense of restriction, for the clever organization of elements and use of perspective create a feeling of extended distance and soaring height.

Daisen-in (Daitoku-ji)

Although a pious tradition associates the construction of this superb karesansui garden with the name of the Muromachi period garden designer Soami, an entry in the biography of the renowned Zen priest Daishô, founder of the Daisen-in, states that he supervised its completion after having collected its rocks himself during the year 1509, and this interpretation seems altogether credible. Confined to a restricted total area of only about one hundred square meters, the garden is composed essentially of several dozen rocks of

A portion of the garden north of the abbot's quarters

Two karesansui gardens divided by the roofed passage

varying shapes, sizes and textures, raked gravel areas, and carefully chosen plants. These elements are ingeniously combined into a superbly integrated arrangement of impressive power and beauty. Although very modest in actual scale, the dynamic composition of the garden creates an impression of great space, and the viewer's imagination is filled with a sense of towering crags, deep hidden valleys swiftly flowing waters, and strangely shaped islands. The whole is permeated with the bold, intuitive spirit of Zen Buddhism, and reveals its symbolic approach toward garden design.

Confined to a brief area, this fine garden has an intimate, cordial atmosphere. It has a kind of pictorial quality about it; a sense of line, color and thrust, and it is known that its designer, Shiken, was a Zen monk whose specialty was painting.

Tôji-in

The garden has been fairly changed from the original pattern, because the buildings have been moved. The tea house and the garden which are said to have been constructed in Muromachi era, are elegant and enjoyable.

The stone arrangement of landscape from the shoin

Reiun-in (Myôshin-ji)

Reiun-in was erected in 1526 and served for a time as a temporary residence for the Emperor Go-Nara. In a narrow area between the shoin and a roofed wall is an exquisite miniature landscape garden, designed by Shiken, a painter in the service of the Shôkoku-ji temple, toward the middle of the sixteenth century. The sure juxtaposition of stones, gravel and foliage into a superb composition reveals clearly the confident eye and artistic awareness of the creator, and this small, but superlative work is one of the finest products of the Zen-inspired aesthetic canons of the late Muromachi period.

Tôji-in

This temple was originally situated atop Mt. Kinugasa. Re-established at its present location in 1338 by Takauji, first of the Ashikaga Shoguns, with the famous monk Musô Soseki as its head abbot, it became the main place of worship for the members of the Ashikaga Family, and contains many important statues of the shoguns of the Ashikaga line. Soseki has traditionally been regarded as the designer of the adjoining gardens but the portion adjoining the Fuyô ("Paradise") pond, north of the hôjô, appears to have been laid out later, during Edo era. However, the ancient pond to the east retains certain features also seen in the Saihô-ji and Tenryû-ji gardens, and may well have been constructed during Soseki's time.

The eastern pond retains layout features of the early Ashikaga period.

Ryôan-ji

A total of fifteen stones make up the entire arrangement, whose ingenious designer is unknown. There are at least three traditional interpretations of the meaning of the garden, but none of them seems entirely convincing, and its true significance remains unclear. Dramatically apparent, however, the unique power of expression and refined aesthetic awareness embodied in its composition.

Ryôan-ji

The stone garden of the Ryôan-ji belongs to a category known as "karesansui" ('dry landscape'), and shows the influence of the Zen Sect of Buddhism in its underlying conceptual approach to garden composition. Laid out on a flat expanse before the abbot's quarters, it consists solely a raked gravel and fifteen rocks of varying sizes, which are arranged in an intermittent sequence which proceeds from left to right. It is surrounded on the south and west by a low wall, roofed with tiles, while a higher wall and gate stand to the east. Not a single tree or shrub grows in this part of the enclosure, and the entire composition is set

Bamboo fence for the tea ceremony house garden named 'Ryôan-ji Gaki'

The broad expanse of white gravel and irregular stones

against the sober background of the thick earth wall. The gravel surface is carefully raked in straight parallel lines except for the areas immediately surrounding the stones, where the lines follow their contours. This form of expression is completely unlike that of conventional gardens; it is spare, abstract, conducive to meditation, and filled with the flavor and perplexities of Zen thought. The Ryôan-ji was originally erected by the powerful daimyo Hosokawa Katsumoto in 1450, but it was burned to the ground shortly after in the destructive Ônin Wars. It is thought that the stone garden postdates the subsequent rebuilding of the temple by his son Masamoto in 1499.

Taizô-in

Fragments of shale are cleverly integrated into a portion of the 'dry falls' seen here. A fine variety of natural rocks are juxtaposed in such a manner that their sizes and textures result in a superb composition marked by a strong pictorial quality.

Taizô-in (Myôshin-ji)

This temple was first erected in 1404 by the daimyo Hatano-Idzumo-no-kami for the Zen priest Muin. The garden is known for its association with the noted painter Kanô Motonobu (1476–1559), who is credited with the present design, which he seems to have executed following the razing of the temple in the Ônin Wars. It is laid out so

The skillfully composed 'dry landscape' garden of the Taizô-in, with the 'central island' in the foreground

that variations in the position of the viewer result in a variety of skillfully arranged compositions, which have a pictorial flavor reminiscent of landscape paintings. The 'dry pond' west of the hôjô is the central point of focus, and includes rock formations representing the mythical islands of Hôrai, a waterfall, and crane islands, which are interrelated through the use of natural stone bridges.

Honpô-ji

In the center front of the "Mitsudomoe" garden, there is a small pond edged by cutting stones which has lotus flowers.

Jukô-in

The garden seen from the hôjô. To the center right is the natural rock bridge which serves as a point of visual focus as well as an essential element in locking the whole arrangement together. Numerous green rocks of modest size give the garden a sensation of softness.

Honpô-ji (Daitoku-ji)

The garden of Honpô-ji was reportedly made by Kôetsu Hon-ami in early Edo period. This is the Plane Karesansui (dry landscape) garden. It has been called "Mitsudomoe" (three "comma" shapes) garden, because it was composed of three islands which took three "comma" forms. The central island has a waterfall.

The stone basin in the west of the shoin, composed by Kôetsu

The focus of the garden structure is the stone bridge which connects two islands.

Jukô-in (Daitoku-ji)

The hedges which form the background are trimmed in an undulating, irregular manner which blends perfectly with the rocks, shrubbery and moss, and the total scene is one of fresh, intense beauty.

The founding of this sub-temple dates to 1566. The famous tea-master Sen no Rikyû received instruction in Zen here, and one tradition attributes the garden to his hand. The garden facing the hôjô is divided into three 'island' groups; the two toward the middle are joined by a ponderous stone bridge which forms the point of central emphasis, an unusual compositional scheme. A dense carpet of moss covers most of the surface of the garden, giving it a natural, rustic feeling.

Sambô-in

View from the Junjôkan

Sambô-in (Daigo-ji)

The Sambô-in, originally known as the Kongôrin-in, is one of the series of complexes that make up the celebrated Daigo-ji temple, founded by the priest Shôbô in 874. The present buildings were erected at the order of Toyotomi Hideyoshi (1536–1598), who held a sumptuous cherry-viewing party and entertainment on the premises in the last year of his life. He is said to have had a hand in the layout of the garden himself, and hurried it to near-completion in about forty days following the great fete, although the final touches and refinements were carried out in the following years under the priest Junkô. The garden is designed to be seen from various points of vantage, either while strolling along the gravel paths or afloat on the broad pond; the central points of emphasis in the majority of views are the island in the middle, with its complex of boulders, trees and shrubs, and the rocks associated with the falls in the background. The sumptuous foliage, impressive dimensions, and rich baroque quality of the garden's arrangement are clear evidence of the representative aesthetic standards of the late sixteenth century. The two large patches of moss building are said to represent a gourd and a sake cup, and are reputed to have been laid out for the flower-viewing extravanza in 1598.

The main area of emphasis in the garden's intricate composition

Daitoku-ji Honbô

The Plane Karesansui garden to the south and the east of the hôjô adds the depth to the concrete garden owing to the borrowed landscape of Higashiyama mountain range.

The waterfall in the south garden

The chain of rock and moss formations in the east ▶
garden

Daitoku-ji Honbô

The Honbô (or Hôjô), administrative headquarters of the Daitoku-ji temple, is bounded on the south and east by superb 'dry landscape' gardens dating to the early seventeenth century. Center of compositional focus in the broad example on the south are two great boulders in the corner, which represent a waterfall. The peaks of Mt. Hiei form an elegant backdrop for the smaller garden to the east, which is composed of a string of low rock and foliage arrangements at the base of a hedge cut into two levels, a feature which reinforces the strong horizontal feeling of the garden. Regarded as a work of the famous garden-designer Kobori Enshû by one tradition, it is more likely that both gardens were laid out by the priest Tenyû in 1636.

Nijô Castle

The garden was composed for the palatial building, Ni-no-Maru. It is so sublime as to be in harmony with the style and the scale of the building.

The view from the grand hall of Ni-no-Maru

From the site of the royal guest house ▶

Nijô Castle, Ni-no-Maru garden

The extensive Ni-no-Maru garden of Nijô Castle is situated south-west of the Great Audience Hall. Although it cannot be accurately dated, it is known to have been complete when the Emperor Go-Mizuno-o paid an imperial visit to the castle in 1626, and it is thought that the master garden-designer, Kobori Enshû remodelled the already-existent gardens on the site in 1624, when a special residence was erected to accomodate the royal presence. The garden is so-arranged that it may be seen to best advantage from the chambers of the Great Hall and the Kuro-shoin, as well as from the south side of the pond, a favorite position for viewing the rock arrangements along the banks.

◀ It is remarkable to use many standing stones both sides of the waterfall so as to show strong tone.

Sentô-Gosho

The garden of the Sentô-Gosho is composed so that all its elements relate harmoniously with, and focus on the central role of the pond. An important factor in achieving this emphasis is the extensive use of areas of grass to accentuate the pond's irregular, natural contours.

Zakke-in

The garden of the abbot's quarter was reportedly built by Nichiren School Abbot, Gyokushin. Gyokushin was one of the priest gardeners who were active in the world of garden composer in Kan-ei era (1624—43). This view is the central part of the garden from the abbot's quarter.

Sentô-Gosho

Constructed for the Emperor Go-Mizuno-o, the Sentô-Gosho was completed in 1628, and it served as his residence from the time of his abdication in the following year until his death in 1680. Its original buildings included a variety of fine structures moved from other sites, such as the special quarters set up for his visit to the Nijô Castle in 1626, but these were destroyed by fire in 1856, and never rebuilt; and today only a few minor structures built in the 'sukiya' style of architecture are to be seen. The term "Sentô" ('Cave of the Sylphs') is taken from classical Chinese literature, as are several other terms by which the compound has been known, and is indicative of the particular interest in Chinese culture which flourished during Edo times. Designed by Kobori Enshû, the garden is filled with a rich profusion of varying scenes and vistas, which unfold as one strolls slowly along its paths.

The broad, gently inclined expanse of carefully selected stones

Zakke-in (Myôshin-ji)

The garden is a Plane Karesansui surrounded by a mud fence. There are several curious stones which indicate sixteen Buddhist Saints (Jûroku-Rakan). The stone arrangement is said to symbolize the Buddhist thought originated in Zen. Though the composer Gyokushin was a Nichiren School priest, he was on intimate terms with Zen monk scholar, Shôshô Hôrin of Rokuon-ji, and even Kobori Enshû.

Harmony between the stone arrangement expressed the Buddhist images and the surrounding plantation

Konchi-in

This fine garden, south of the hôjô, is known traditionally as the "Tsuru-Kame-no-niwa" (Crane-Tortoise

Garden) because of the two chief features in its arrangement, the formation representing a tortoise, to the left, and the crane group, opposite it, to the right.

"Tortoise Island" symbolizes the negative.

Konchi-in (Nanzen-ji)

Each group of the Crane-Tortoise Garden (above) is located in front of a high, irregularly shaped hedge which harmonizes with and complements the total composition very successfully.

Originally situated at Takagamine, northwest of Kyoto, this temple was re-established on the present site in 1605 by Sûden, one of Tokugawa Ieyasu's advisors. Kobori

"Crane Island" symbolizes the positive.

Enshû was called on to plan the layout of the buildings and gardens; and although his name is associated with a number of Kyoto gardens, this is the sole example of the master's renowned prowess in garden design for which there is irrefutable documentary evidence. Work was begun on the compound in 1627, and its completion seems to have taken four to five years.

Nanzen-ji

According to tradition, this garden is said to be the symbolic representation of a tiger and its cubs crossing a river. Immaculate white gravel, carefully raked, covers the majority of the broad area, and serves to focus attention

on the dramatic arrangement of rocks, trees and shrubs in the left hand corner. Kyoto is filled with superlative "karesansui" gardens, and this is certainly among the finest.

Nanzen-ji

Founded in 1291, when the Emperor Kameyama's detached palace was converted into a temple, the buildings of this great Zen temple have been leveled on two occasions by disastrous fires. The hôjô, formerly a part of the Seiryôden Palace, was dismantled, moved, and re-erected on its present site in 1611. To its south is a superb garden. Unusual in its extensive use of raked gravel, it is said to have been designed by Kobori Enshû at the same time he was working on the Konchi-in garden, nearby. The variety of trees and shrubs used, and the diversity of shapes into which they have been trimmed and formed, constitutes another distinctive feature.

The view from the veranda of hôjô

Jôju-in

(All over view of Jôju-in garden)

Jôju-in (Kiyomizu Temple)

This beautifully maintained garden adjoins the Honbô of the Kiyomizu Temple, extending from the northeast of the structure around to the west. Soami and Enshû have both been credited with its design, although no historical records exist to substantiate these traditions. Nevertheless, the ingenious manner in which the garden has been laid out, its beautiful harmony, and the impressive way in which the hill-slopes in the background have been utilized in the

The gardens view from the flower shaped window of Shoin

The "Ebôshi (hat) rock" and the waterfall in the central island. The water is flowing from the spring at the foot of the hill.

total composition is evidence that the designer was a man of considerable talent. A handbook for garden construction published in 1716 mentions the garden, and it appears likely that it was completed sometime during the latter half of the previous century. This garden is particularly well suited for moon-viewing because of its orientation, for the moon rises over the hills to the rear and reflects perfectly in the pond.

Shinju-an

The temple has three gardens. The most famous one is the dry landscape garden in the east of the hôjô which is popularly known as "Seven, Five, Three" garden. The name of "Seven, Five, Three" comes from the number of stones arranged in the long and narrow garden. The number is said to express happiness and good fortune.

The main entrance to the hôjô

The lovely 'Seven, Five, Three' garden east of the hōjō

The stone arrangement of the front garden of the guest pavilion

Shinju-an (Daitoku-ji)

Founded by the famous Zen priest Ikkyu in 1429, and destroyed during the disastrous Ônin Wars, the present hôjô dates to the year 1636. The engagingly off-hand garden to the east of the building is situated in a long narrow space before a hedge. Known as the 'Seven, Five, Three' garden because of the number of stones in its three groups, it has an intimate, cordial quality about it that is very refreshing. The shoin structure north of the hôjô was moved from the Imperial Palace to its present site in 1638. Behind it is a famous tea-house, the Teigyokken, and a modest, refined garden laid out in a manner which reflects the canons of taste associated with the tea ceremony. The designers of both gardens are unknown.

Kohô-an

The elegant gardens of this temple extend from the area adjoining the hôjô to the environs of the shoin. The portion facing the 'Bôsen' Tea Ceremony room (right) is regarded as particularly fine, along with the splendid garden outside the shoin (above), the composition of which is said to have been inspired by the "Eight Views of the River Hsiang", a famous series of Chinese land-scape scenes. The 'Bôsen' Tea Ceremony room is built in the shoin style. It has large paper shôji fitted above, so that the spectator's view is confined to a horizontal area, an arrangement visually reminiscent of the view from the window of a boat. When a tea ceremony is held in this room, the participants rinse their hands in the stone basin to the right, and enter through the low opening beneath the shôji.

▲ Inner tea ceremony
garden of the tea room
'Bôsen'

Hand washing spot and
tea ceremony garden of
'Chokunyû-ken'

72

Kohô-an (Daitoku-ji)

This temple was originally erected by Kobori Enshû in 1612 in the compound of the Ryûkô-in, but the location later proved to be too restricted in size and the Kohô-an was moved to its present site. The original plan was composed of a series of fine buildings, and included a Tea Ceremony structure named the 'Bôsen'. Enshû was at the height of his creative powers when he directed the construction and layout of this temple, and its completion marks one of his most important contributions to the culture of the early Edo period. The present buildings were erected after a disastrous fire leveled the temple in 1793. This project was carried out by Matsudaira Fumai, a follower of the Tea Ceremony canons established by Enshû. The new buildings were constructed in strict accordance with Enshû's ideas and taste, and the present architecture, disposition, and details of the Kohô-an seem to accurately reflect the master's early seventeenth century plan. The choice of the three character name Kohô-an for the temple is of particular interest. The first character (ko) means solitary or alone, while the second (hô) signifies the thatched roof covering traditionally seen on peasant sampans, and by extension, one of these small craft itself. The last character (an) means a retreat or hermitage. The name might thus be translated as the "Hermitage of the Solitary Sampan", and it is not surprising that many aspects of the adjoining gardens are suggestive of water landscapes in their appearance. It seems that the designer wished that visitors, when gazing out at the garden, would have the impression that they were actually afloat (see color photos, p.70, 71).

Nishi-Honganji
A karesansui (dry landscape) example dating to late Momoyama or early Edo times.

Shûon-an

The dramatic stone formation in the northeast corner of the garden which symbolizes a group of lofty mountain peaks. The hedge in the rear is trimmed low so that the distant rooftops of Kyoto and the Kizu River may be seen, along with the Higashiyama hills in the background.

Nishi-Honganji

Among the stone groups (P.74) are crane and tortoise 'islands', related through the use of a gently arched bridge, and three boulders representing a waterfall, which stand to the rear. The palms add a baroque touch to the complicated arrangement.

The sumptuous Dai-shoin structure of this temple is said to have originally been part of Hideyoshi's Fushimi-Momoyama palace, donated to the Nishi-Honganji by the shogun, Tokugawa Iemitsu, in 1630 and set up on its present site two years later. According to this tradition, all of the essential elements from the original garden were removed and transported to the new location. However, a conflicting opinion contends that the shoin was first built in 1632, and if this is the case, the style of the garden must be taken to represent that current during early Edo times rather than the manner fashionable during the Momoyama period.

The stone arrangement on the east garden of the hôjô

Shûon-an (Ikkyû Temple)

This temple is popularly known as the "Ikkyû-ji", as the celebrated Zen priest Ikkyû Sôjun (1394–1481) spent his last years here. It was erected by Ikkyû in 1455 in memory of the celebrated scholar and priest Shômyô. There are three gardens in the precincts: the "Tiger's-mound Garden", the fine example in front of Ikkyû's chapel, and the hôjô garden. They represent different 'dry landscape' arrangements, and probably date to the early Edo period in their present forms. The point of emphasis in the northeast corner of the hôjô garden is shown in the photograph.

◀ Center of compositional focus — the bridge and "waterfall" boulders

Manshu-in

Center of focus in the lovely Manshu-in "dry landscape" garden in front of the Ko-shoin

All over view from east high ground of the Ko-shoin

Hand washing water container of the Ko-shoin

80

Manshu-in

This temple belongs to the Tendai sect of Buddhism, and a member of a noble family related to the Imperial House has traditionally served as its head priest. Originally situated at a site close to Yoshimitsu's Kitayama villa (Kinkaku), it was transferred to the present location by Prince Yoshihisa in 1656. Its main buildings are superbly designed and furnished, and show numerous points of similarity to the Katsura Rikyû. The temple's 'karesansui' garden displays the refined taste of Yoshihisa, who is revered for his patronage of the arts and interest in the Tea Ceremony and garden design.

Chishaku-in

This superb garden is traditionally thought to have been inspired by the mountain landscape at Lu-shan in China. A fall tumbles dramatically down the steep slope which rises just opposite the shoin. Variously trimmed hedges and boulders of contrasting shapes cover the hillside, and present a scene which is unique in the originality of its conception.

Gyokuhô-in

Laid out in a crisp, geometrical manner, this enclosure has a spacious formality about it. It adjoins the Bishô-an and Gyokuhô-Zengû structures to the left, and is noted for the fine harmony of skillfully matched flagstones in its paths and the carefully raked patterns in the intervening gravel areas.

Chishaku-in

There are a number of landmarks associated with Toyo-tomi Hideyoshi in the Higashiyama-Shichijô neighborhood, and the site now occupied by the Chishaku-in was formerly the location of the Jôun-ji, a temple erected by Hideyoshi in order to gain religious merit for his first son, Tsurumatsu, who died while he was still a small child. The Chishaku-in had been part of the extensive Negoro temple complex in Kii Province, which was destroyed by Hideyoshi in 1585 because of the opposition of its soldier-monks to his plans. After his death, however, the Chishaku-in was re-estab-lished on its present site by the priest Genyû, in 1601. The unusual garden was laid out in 1674 by Unshô, seventh abbot of the temple, and one of its unique features is the pond, which extends under the shoin, and thus creates the impression that the structure is a "tsuridono", a kind of pavilion usually built out over lakes.

The view of the waterfall and the artificial mountain from the shoin

Outside the 'founder's hall'

Gyokuhô-in (Myôshin-ji)

The founding of the Myôshin-ji dates to the year 1335, when the Emperor Hanazono took the tonsure and converted part of his palace premises into a small Zen temple. The priest Keigen was installed as abbot, and the building complex in which the retired emperor devoted himself to the study of Zen was named the Gyokuhô-in ("Hall of the Jade Phoenix"). The temple was destroyed by fire during the Ônin Wars and the two main buildings in the compound dated to much later times: the Bishô-an is a sixteenth century structure transferred from the Tôfuku-ji, and the Gyokuhô-Zengû was erected in 1656. Stylized and formal in its composition, the karesansui garden (color photo P.83) is thought to be product of the middle Edo period, completed about 1720.

Kanju-ji

The hedge in the middleground serves to integrate the grass-covered area to the front with the portions of the garden centered on the broad lake in the rear, and to create a greater sense of dimension, space, and compositional order.

Entsû-ji

Noted for the unusual horizontal stress of its composition, the Entsû-ji garden is made up of low formations of rocks of various hues, set up on a gently rolling surface covered by deep moss, and backed by a low straight hedge.

An usual decorative stone basin outside the guest house

Kanju-ji

A temple was first established at this location in 900 in accordance with the wishes of the Emperor Daigo, and the landscape garden, with its broad pond, still retains certain features of composition which are typical of Heian period gardens. Among these are the central island, symbolic of the "Abode of the Immortals", and the arrangement of the pond, which is laid out so that the garden is seen to advantage while afloat, a feature which reveals the great popularity of 'boating excursions' among Heian nobility. The small garden just in front of the shoin is noted for its refinement and originality. Laid out during the Edo period, it is admired for the fine manner in which the pond landscape in the background has been utilized to complement its own visual order and sense of space.

Entsû-ji

The layout and disposition of the garden have been skillfully planned so that distant Mt. Hiei forms an integral part of the totality, a particularly effective example of the 'borrowed-view' technique of garden design.

The Emperor Go-Mizuno-o had country villas set up at a series of sites before he finally settled on the Shûgakuin location in 1655, and one of these, the Hatae-Goten, stood on the grounds currently occupied by the Entsû-ji. The original arrangement of the villa is unclear, but it appears to have included two or three structures constructed in the 'sukiya' style. After the Shûgakuin site was decided on for the retired monarch's villa, the Hatae-Goten grounds were given to the Konoe Family, and subsequently re-established as a nunnery and named the Entsû-ji. The shoin is said to have once been a building in the Imperial Palace, transferred to the temple in 1678, and the garden is thought to date from that time.

Rocks of contrasting colors and textures are ingeniously utilized in the garden's arrangement.

Tôkai-an

The garden of the shoin has three artificial mountains which express holy islands. While, it has the stone arrangement which is composed of three holy stones.

Fumon-in

A path divides this garden into two. The sharp contrast between these two realms suggests the contradictions which constitute an important aspect of Zen thought.

▲ The garden of the white Roji in front of hôjô

Karesansui inner garden sur-
▼rounded by shoin and hôjô

Tôkai-an (Myôshin-ji)

The garden of the shoin composed by priest Tôboku of Kaizô-ji Temple in 1814 (late Tokugawa Era). The original blue-print of the garden has remained and it keeps on record that the garden has three holy islands. The stone arrangement of three holy stones shows the composer's wish for the eternal prosperity of Buddhism. Tôkai-an has two other gravel and stone gardens.

The provocative juxtaposition of boulders, shrubs and raked gravel

Fumon-in (Tôfuku-ji)

The great Zen monastery Tôfuku-ji was founded by the noble Fujiwara Michiie in 1236, with the priest Shôitsu as its first abbot. A number of superb buildings are situated in the extensive grounds, and the 'founder's hall' compound contains an interesting garden which is unique in its arrangement (color photo P.91). Divided into a flat gravel area in which plain bands are alternated with raked ones; and a slope crowded with a profusion of shrubs, trees and boulders, complemented by a small pool, this garden has a surprisingly contemporary feeling in its composition. It is thought to date to the middle seventeenth century.

Murin-an

A fresh, sparkling stream flows down through the grass-covered meadow clearing of this broad garden, which is laid out in a typical Meiji period "natural" style. A fan-shaped interval is left open in the surrounding enclosure of trees in order to reveal the Higashiyama hills in the background.

95

Murin-an

The villa, Murin-an was built in 1895, and the garden was composed by famous gardener Jihei Ogawa under the instruction of the owner Aritomo Yamagata. The garden is bright and soft. It has also European mood.

The three steps
waterfall
in a grove

CONTENTS

THE BEGINNINGS OF JAPANESE GARDENS

The earliest historical reference to the construction of a garden in Japan is contained in a passage in the *Nihon-shoki* ("Chronicles of Japan"), an important work compiled early in the eighth century. According to the account, a man with the unusual name of Roji-no-Takumi arrived with a group of immigrants from the Korean Kingdom of Paekche about 606, during the reign of the Empress Suiko. He is described as a specialist in the art of erecting miniature replicas of Mt. Sumeru, the great mountain which lies at the center of the Buddhist universe; and he is credited with the completion of an artificial hill of this type, with a connecting bridge, in an enclosure south of the imperial residence. Although the details of its shape and layout are not precisely known, scholary opinion is inclined to regard this enigmatic mound as a primitive but important ancestor of the splendid landscape gardens that constitute such an important aspect of Japanese culture.

About 620, a garden was completed within the palace of Soga-no-Umako, an important dignitary and early patron of Buddhism, and it is described as having a man-made pond with an artificial island in the middle. This unusual landscape feature seems to have captured the fancy of Umako's contemporaries, who are known to have referred to him by the engaging appellation "Shima-no-Otodo"("Great Minister of the Island") after its completion. The concept of an island as an essential feature of a landscape garden seems to have been established about this time, and it is interesting that the word 'shima' (island) was used to connote the idea of a garden (along with the terms in present-day use, 'sono' and 'niwa') up until about the end of the eighth century.

Although the many spacious gardens laid out before the ninth century exist today only in historical and literary sources, there is sufficient evidence to show that their chief characteristic was a pond or lake, the shoreline of which was designed in imitation of the rough, windswept scenery adjacent to the ocean.

Rocks and boulders were combined skillfully to create a variety of pleasant inlets, promontories, and interesting contour changes along the water's edge, and various species of water birds seem to have added a lively grace to such scenes. Lyric descriptions of these gardens, with their water vistas, islands and rocky shores are contained in the *Manyôshû,* a superb anthology of poetry compiled about 759. By the eighth century, ships were plying the rough waters separating Japan from the continent with some frequency. Members of the nobility and priesthood made the perilous crossing to China in some numbers during this period, bringing back with them many elements of the superlative culture then flourishing under the T'ang Dynasty. A by-product of this historic intercourse was the growth of interest in marine scenery of the sort encountered on these journeys, which appears to have made such a lasting impression on the travellers that they wished to re-create similar landscapes in their gardens, where they could be contemplated and enjoyed at leisure during the course of daily life. The use of white sand and small pebbles, as well as boulders weathered into unusual shapes by wind and water, as a means of heightening the sensation of the presence of the sea dates from this early period.

With the establishment of the new capital, Heian-kyô (present-day Kyoto) in 794 at a site in Yamashiro some twenty-odd miles north of Nara, the former capital, progress in garden design gained increasing momentum. The Nara period (710–784) pre-occupation with seascape elements became an established, traditional feature in the main gardens designed during Heian times (784–1185), irrespective of whether they were constructed in connection with Buddhist temple complexes, palace grounds, or villa locations.

Although the essential features of garden design continued, basically unchanged, over the following centuries, a gradual process of refinement and specialization took place. The earlier conception of simply re-creating some vague, general sense of a sea vista was modified, and particular, characteristic elements of certain well-known locales came to be used as models or departure points in the layout of gardens. Thus, certain aspects of the wind-sculptured crags of Shiogama and the lovely pine-covered islets of Matsushima were created in miniature in the Kawara-in garden of Minamoto-no-Tôru (822–895); and the Rokujô-in of Onakatomi Sukechika (954–1038) contained a garden composed after the famous Ama-no-hashidate sandspit in Tango Province. During these centuries of development and refinement many changes occurred. Nevertheless, the basic inspiration for garden composition continued to be drawn from scenes associated with the sea, irrespective of the size of the garden, and the design canons which evolved from this source were of basic importance in the evolution of the main layout theme characteristic of classic examples of later ages – the combination of an artificial mountain, bordered by a spring-fed pond.

KYOTO AND GARDENS

The importance of Kyoto's role as the capital city and chief center of culture in Japan for over a thousand years is clearly revealed by the many noteable gardens, which range in date from the Heian period (784–1185) to the first years of the twentieth century, that are preserved at various locations in and around the city today. Although their total amounts to a sizeable figure, and no other vicinity in Japan can boast of a number which is even close to being comparable, it is only proper to point out that they represent only a portion of the multitude of fine gardens constructed in the area since the ninth century, for the devastating wars and all too frequent conflagrations that mark Kyoto's history have caused the destruction of a great many splendid examples. Nevertheless, the impressive array which has survived is apt testimony of the great outlay of labor, expense, and creative effort that has resulted from the habitual passion for gardens which is a traditional characteristic of the residents of Kyoto.

The Kyoto environs have been favored generously by nature. Mountains with thick stands of timber rise on three sides, and a profusion of springs, streams and rivers supply a yearlong abundance of water; low, forested foothills rise at irregularly-spaced intervals, forming a pleasant patchwork of hue and contour with the neighboring ponds, embankments, and neat fields. This rich setting has produced all of the materials necessary for garden construction since early times – varieties of shrubs and trees, mosses and grass, as well as pebbles, sand and boulders. Furthermore, the multiplicity of such components, available close-by, has always afforded the Kyoto garden designer with distinct creative advantages – a wide freedom of choice in the elements he used in his works and considerable latitude in the manner he laid them out. Among the gardens of particular interest in Kyoto and its suburbs are those at the following locations:

Heian period (784–1185)
1) Hôô-dô (Byôdô-in)
2) Saga-Gosho
3) Shinsen-en
4) Hôkongô-in
5) Jôruri-ji

Yoshino period (1336–1392)
1) Saihô-ji
2) Tenryû-ji
3) Nanzen-in
4) Tôji-in

Muromachi period (1392–1568)
1) Rokuon-ji ("Kinkaku-ji")
2) Jishô-ji ("Ginkaku-ji")
3) Daisen-in shoin
4) Reiun-in
5) Ryôan-ji hôjô

Momoyama period (1568–1615)
1) Sambô-in (Daigo-ji)
2) Taizô-in
3) Jukô-in

Early Edo period (1615–c. 1750)
1) Nishi-Hongan-ji, daishoin
2) Konchi-in
3) Nanzen-ji hôjô
4) Katsura Rikyû
5) Kohô-an
6) Shôsei-en
7) Kôdai-ji
8) Shûon-an
9) Shûgakuin Rikyu
10) Manshu-in
11) Chôfuku-ji
12) En-an
13) Chion-in
14) Honpô-ji
15) Shisen-dô
16) Zakke-in
17) Omote-Senke
18) Ura-Senke
19) Shôren-in

Late Edo period (c. 1750–1867)
1) Entsû-ji
2) Chishaku-in
3) Gyokuhô-in
4) Myôshin-ji honbô
5) Tôkai-an
6) Kankyû-an
7) Horiuchi residence
8) Hisada residence
9) Keishun-in

Meiji period (1868–1912)
1) Murin-an
2) Seifû-sô
3) Ichida residence
4) Heian Shrine

Although modifications in composition, scale and arrangement have taken place in some of these works with the passing of time, all of them retain certain essential features which were embodied into their original plans. As one might suspect, the older gardens have generally changed to a larger degree than the ones completed in more recent times. This is a natural consequence of the rebuilding which has occurred frequently at early temple and palace sites. Many other gardens have fared less well, and lie in half-ruin, or survive only in some brief portion, such as a section of a rock arrangement, which may have been incorporated into a later rebuilding. In addition, there are descriptions in historical documents of a group of noted gardens which have now entirely disappeared.

Early historical accounts mention the presence of an influential clan named the Hata in the basin-plain (the "Kadono" area) that was chosen some centuries later as the site for the great capital city of Heian. The Hata appears to have arrived by way of the Korean Peninsula from China about the third century, and are credited with the introduction of agricultural and distilling techniques, sericulture, weaving, and other features of the advanced culture of the continent. Descriptions mention that they were also responsible for projects such as the damming of the Oikawa (the Katsura river), an accomplishment that suggests the extent of their power and ability at organization. The great benefactor of Buddhism, Prince Shôtoku, died in 621, and in the following year Hata Kawakatsu, leader of the clan, founded the Kôryû-ji temple (known first as the "Kadono-no-Hata-dera") in order to pray for the repose of the prince's soul, at a location on the east bank of the Katsura river.

Various bits of evidence reveal the growing authority and importance of this clan in these early centuries, and it appears that the Emperor Kammu's decision to establish a new capital in this area in 793 seems to have been based in part on the transfer of extensive tracts of land in the area to the court by the Hata family. Furthermore, the wife of the Chief Commissioner of Works in charge of the construction of the capital was the daughter of a prominent member of the clan, and the site adopted for the Imperial Palace buildings is traditionally thought to have been the location of Hata Kawakatsu's residence.

The location chosen for the capital is a broad, gently sloping plain, bounded on the east by the Kamo River and the west by the Katsura; and surrounded by mountains of moderate height on three sides, the south being open. At the end of the low mountain chain on the east, the Uji and Kizu Rivers cut across, flowing toward the south-west, forming a natural line of demarcation across the wide lower perimeter of the plain. Political considerations were undoubtedly an important factor in settling on this site, but the convenience of communication, with a series of roads radiating out to the provinces, and rivers large enough to support fair-sized boats, provided practical advantages which certainly influenced the decision. At the same time, it is difficult to imagine that the natural beauties of the setting, sheltered by a protective ring of mountains covered with luxuriant stands of timber, and graced by a copious supply of springs and clear rivers, were not significant elements in the choice, as well.

These natural features have continued to be one of Kyoto's greatest assets throughout the centuries. There is some justification, however, in imagining that they have never appeared to greater advantage than during the early ninth century, when the great capital city, laid out on a grand scale in the form of a rectangle intersected by broad avenues, was first brought to completion. Patterned, as had been the Heijô capital at Nara, after the Chinese capital of Ch'ang-an during the Sui dynasty, the city stretched roughly three and a half miles from north to south, and three miles east to west; and a low earth wall and exterior moat marked its boundaries. A wide thoroughfare led north from the main entrance gate to the city, which faced south in accordance with Chinese ideas, dividing the metropolis neatly into eastern and western precincts. It terminated to the north in the palace enclosure, measuring about one mile by three-quarters, which contained the imperial quarters, the highest administrative and ceremonial halls of state, and residential apartments for the nobility and important functionaries.

Situated in the middle of this flat plain with it abundance of running water, and surrounded by the dark green of neighboring forests, the broad expanse of the capital, with its orderly, checker-board pattern, accented by the emerald-blue tiles of the palace roofs and the towering pagodas of temple compounds, must have presented a scene of restrained harmony, an altogether serene fusion of the creative efforts of man and the gracious elements provided by a bountiful nature.

During the early Heian period, many fine gardens were built in which the distinctive topographical features of the area were utilized with particular success, such as the examples at the Reizen-in, Junwa-in, Suzaku-in, Saga-in, and Shinsen-en. The latter was laid out as a pleasure park for the court, and the Emperor Kammu and his cortege first paid a visit to the grounds in the year 800. It appears to have covered an extensive area to the south of the palace enclosure (roughly 33 acres), and the natural features within the garden seem to have been skillfully utilized in its total composition. According to a diagram of the garden drawn in later times, water flowed from a natural spring in the northeast, across the grounds, finally to spill into a broad pond with an island situated in its center. The water supply from the robust spring seems to have supplied an abundance of water for this pond, and it probably did not go dry even in times of drought. It seems apparent therefore, that admiration for the spring accounts for the name Shinsen-en ("Sacred Spring Garden"). The garden was the scene of frequent religious ceremonies designed to appeal to the gods for rain during the Heian period, and the plentiful supply of water undoubtedly resulted in its choice as an appropriate location for such rites.

Deer and wild birds were propagated in large numbers in the Shinsen-en, and stalking them seems to have been a popular form of court recreation. In its general atmosphere of wildlife, running water, and groves of trees, it is apparent that the basic objective in laying out the vast complex was to re-create a vivid, lifelike sense of authentic nature. At the same time, however, various buildings, which contributed a sense of balance and refinement to the composition, revealed the fact that its essential purpose was to serve as a place of recreation for the court members. Chief structure among these was the Kanrinkaku, a storied pavilion with attached wings. Other buildings designed for "fishing" and "waterfall contemplation" were situated close to the perimeter of the pond in appropriate locations. Many rock formations were erected at carefully chosen spots adjacent to the water's edge as well as in the pond, a project carried out under the direction of Kose-no-Kanaoka, the chief official in charge of the Shinsen-en, according to an account in an ancient document, the *Shugaisho*.

The Shinsen-en was maintained in good order until the middle of the Heian period, but its subsequent history is a dreary one. As the Imperial House gradually lost its political power, the fortunes of the great garden waned. Uncared for over the years, its fine trees and shrubs disappeared, and modifications in the city's street plan and the building of houses reduced its area to a small portion of the original size. A small pond, just south of Nijô Castle, is all that remains today of the once spacious grounds; unfortunately it provides little evidence of the splendid atmosphere of the ninth century composition.

An extensive palace (the Saga-in) was built for the Emperor Saga (r. 809–823) following his abdication, at a site west of Heian which is known to the present day for its scenic beauty. He took up residence in the splendid buildings, built in the "shinden" style, in 834, and lived there until his death. In 876, the compound was re-established as a Buddhist temple and given the name Daikaku-ji. It is known that the temple grounds spread over almost one hundred acres, and it is surmised that the palace complex and its garden must have been laid out on a grand scale, and covered a considerable area.

Considering the wars and fires which have caused extensive damage to Kyoto on repeated occasions, it is not surprising that little remains of the many great gardens laid out in the area during the early part of the Heian period, well over a thousand years ago. Only a single site retains enough of its original form and arrangement to give one an idea of the canons of landscape gardening current at the time – the location where the Saga-in stood, adjacent to Ôsawa pond in the Daikaku-ji precincts. Hills rise up just to the rear, and these formed a natural backdrop for the palace, which looked out over the broad, gently rolling contours of the Saga plains to the south and the heights of Arashiyama and the Katsura river in the distance. Some idea of the original scale of the huge complex may be gained by a brief glance at Ôsawa pond, which covers more than eight acres. It contains two islands, situated close to the north shore. About one hundred meters north of the pond are the remnants of a rock composition, which seems to have been situated some distance below the mouth of a waterfall, along the stream that supplied water to the pond. Many boulders and rocks of a size and shape appropriate for garden layout now lie hidden below the surface of neighboring fields, and it is thought that they were probably components of the ninth century arrangement. Although the details of the original garden have long since disappeared, enough of the general features of the pond and its surroundings remain to provide the visitor with some sense of the splendid composition of the original. There is little controversy about the beauty of the location and the natural setting certainly must have created an atmosphere which complemented the garden in every way.

Saionji Kintsune (1171–1244), an important court noble of the early Kamakura period, had a villa erected in the northwestern outskirts of Kyoto, which he named the Kitayamatei. The location seems to have been admired for the beauty of its setting from Heian times, and the third Ashikaga Shogun, Yoshimitsu (1358–1408), a man of great refinement who took greater pleasure in the arts than in administration, had a splendid villa (the "Kitayamadono", or "Kinkaku"), built for himself on the premises, where he spent the last years of his life. Closeby is the Ryôan-ji temple, established by Hosokawa Katsumoto (1430–1473), one of the principal figures in the internecine Ônin Wars which resulted in the destruction of the greater part of the city.

Yoshimasa (1435–1490), eighth of the Ashikaga Shoguns, is remembered as a patron and connoisseur of the arts, and his

Higashiyama villa (which included the Ginkaku, "Silver Pavilion") served as a gathering place for the most renowned poets, playwrights, painters, and other men of taste of the period. Yoshimasa's fondness for gardens was little short of an obsession, and he is known to have devoted considerable effort and time to investigating promising sites before he finally settled on the location at the foot of the Higashiyama hills already occupied by the Jôdo-ji temple for his superb villa-retreat. The distinctive beauty of the area, with its cool springs, year-round abundance of fresh water, and thick stands of trees, make it an ideal villa site, and the splendid garden, with its fine pond and celebrated Ginkaku structure attests to Yoshimasa's discriminating taste and sense of arrangement.

No one who visits the several gardens mentioned above can fail to be impressed by the appropriateness of their settings and the profound sense of natural beauty which characterizes each in its own distinctive manner. Each is a harmonious total composition, a skillful blending of the garden designer's best efforts with the inherent advantages present at the location.

It is clear from these, and the multitude of other lovely gardens in the city of Kyoto and its environs, that the wealth of views and natural scenic features which grace and enrich the area have served as a constant inspiration for garden compositon, as well as an essential factor in their success as works of art.

It has already been mentioned that the ancient gardens of Japan were more or less direct imitations of natural landscapes. With the passing of time, however, concepts of garden design advanced, and a more complex sense of choice and arrangement in layout gradually developed. A greater range of elements was introduced into garden composition, and an aesthetic canon based on the juxtaposition and arrangement of compositional elements into an integrated totality gradually emerged. Kyoto was the main locale for this development, and it is obvious that the distinctive characteristics of the local climate and landscape, with its rocks, trees and other natural features shaped and influenced this progress in many ways.

Kyoto is situated on a gently-inclined plain, enclosed by a horseshoe-shaped perimeter of low mountains, open only on the south. From a climatic standpoint, it is far from ideal, for the surrounding mountains cut off the winds in summer, resulting in a high, constant humidity, and act to preserve the penetrating cold which marks the long winter season. During the summer, when the humidity generally continues through the night, the climate is particularly enervating, a condition which has given rise to the practice of utilizing water in a variety of ways to mitigate the heat. Thus, networks of canals have been constructed in various parts of the city (a testimony to the copious supply of water in the area), and it has been customary in Kyoto since Heian times to channel water from rivers and springs, and direct its flow through gardens, close to dwellings. This practice, known as 'yari-mizu', creates an atmosphere of coolness by its sound, as well as actually relieving the humidity through the presence of running water, and there are frequent references to it in the *Tale of Genji* and *Makura-no-Sôshi,* literary works of the Heian period. Such artificial streams were installed in the gardens laid out in conjunction with the splendid residences of the nobility, the buildings of which were erected in an architectural style known as 'shinden-zukuri', a distinctive form of single-storied, unpainted construction, with shingled roofs. The ground plans for such buildings varied, and different subsidiary structures were connected to the oblong main building by veranda corridors. Orientation was invariably toward the south, facing a broad garden which had running water as an integral feature.

Standard practice seems to have been to draw water from a source on the north side of the complex, direct its flow under the raised veranda-corridor leading from the main building to subsidiary living quarters on the east, and then have it run in a meandering course past the main chamber, finally to empty into a spacious pond. Unlike the practice in earlier times, rocks were used sparingly, and set up only at those few locations along the course of the stream where they were thought to be necessary as points of visual emphasis. In laying out such gardens, the main objective was to reproduce the atmosphere of natural fields, and the stream usually flowed in a circuitous, dilatory manner between gentle knolls covered with pampas grass and wild flowers. During Heian times, the fresh green moors of Murasakino and Saga lay close by the outskirts of the city, and their beauty provided an ever-present source of inspiration for garden design. The nobility of the period enjoyed frequent excursions to the surrounding countryside, where they delighted in listening to the pleasant sounds of birds and insects, and searching for wild flowers. Their fondness for this sylvan atmosphere is clearly revealed in their preoccupation with accurately reproducing it in their gardens.

In addition to utilizing fashioned streams ('yari-mizu') to alleviate the enervating humidity characteristic of Kyoto summers, it was only natural that the many springs and natural ponds in the area constituted attractive locations where one might find some relief from the stifling heat. Consequently, it is not surprising that the nobles of Heian times appropriated the best of these sites for certain of their residences. Palace-garden complexes of this sort were known as 'Izumi-dono' ("Spring Palace"), or 'Sui-kaku' ("Water Pavilion"), and the palace of the Emperor Shirakawa, and the residences of the Minister of the Right, Minamoto Morofusa (known as the Kuga-suikaku) at Rokujô, and Minamoto Masanaga (the Hachijô-suikaku) are representative examples.

No point of visual focus is more important in the organization of a traditional garden than the waterfall, and an interesting Heian period document, the *Sakutei-ki* ("Notes on Garden Design") lists ten different varieties, additional evidence of the considerable repetoire of arrangement features developed by garden designers during Heian times. The noteable progress made in constructing waterfalls and channeling water in this period may be explained in large part as representing the influence of the topography of the Kyoto basin, for the close contiguity of low mountains on three sides provided the natural features essential for this development.

Among early garden waterfalls, two noted works should be mentioned: the one built in connection with the Hôkongo-in, which was completed in 1130 in the Hanazono area, and another fashioned in a hillside behind the garden of the Kitayamatei villa of Saionji Kintsune, which was described by a contemporary poet, Sadaie, as being forty-five feet in height. It is obvious that great care was always exercised in arranging a waterfall and its associated boulders because of its importance as a primary point of focus in garden composition. The finest stones were selected for the rock formation bordering the fall, and considerable time and effort were devoted to studying the most appropriate manner for the water to descend. Thus, the categories of falls mentioned in the *Sakutei-ki* are differentiated on the basis of the manner in which water actually falls – in a broad torrent, like a thin thread, laterally, or divided into two streams. Furthermore, the sounds of falls were subject to particular scrutiny, and the rocks at the bottom were chosen so that the impact of the water on them created an acoustic quality in harmony with the total composition.

Another renowned waterfall is the example in the garden of the Sambô-in of the Daigo-ji temple. During the Keichô period (1596–1615) this garden was modified and improved by the abbot Gien from time to time, and he is said to have had the noted garden designer Kentei re-arrange the rock formations of the waterfall on repeated occasions before they met his satisfaction.

The plenitude of hills, knolls and rocky promontories which surround Kyoto provided a fine choice of inclines and cliffs for the construction of waterfalls, and it is not surprising that this aspect of garden layout reached an impressive level of achievement locally, and has exerted a continual influence on garden composition in other regions of Japan since Heian times.

In traditional garden design, two factors were always given basic consideration: the use of the best natural features and topographical variations of the site, and the most effective utilization of scenery in the distance so that it might be drawn into, and employed successfully in the total composition of the garden. Although many Kyoto gardens show the realization of these objectives, space allows only the mention of a few. The beautifully preserved example at the Byôdô-in, originally the palace residence of Fujiwara Yorimichi (992–1074) should be noted first. Yorimichi rose to the post of Regent, and entertained the Emperor on the premises, which are located along the quiet Uji River, facing a splendid mountain vista which rises steeply above the far shore. Ashikaga Yorimitsu's Kitayama-dono (Kinkaku) palace was set against the dark green mass of Mt. Kinugasa, with its gently curving outline, and this backdrop has been beautifully utilized in the composition. Possibly the finest example of the realization of these ideals is the Shûgakuin villa. From the vantage point of the Rin-un-tei, situated on the highest level of the garden ('Kami-chaya'), a superb panorama stretches out before the viewer, ranging from the mountains of Kurama which loom up to the right, across the Ohara valley and on to the Nishiyama range in the distance. This superb view is a perfectly integrated element in the abstract composition of the great garden, and it provides a sense of space and scale which is altogether unique. The culmination of man's efforts to harmonize his own creative vision with the finest features of his natural surroundings are eminently apparent in such gardens.

BUDDHISM AND GARDENS

In the history of landscape garden design in Japan, many of the superb developments which mark the progress achieved over the centuries can be traced to the influence of Buddhist thought. Evidence of this influence may be seen as early as the Asuka period, when an immigrant from the Korean kingdom of Paekche named Roji-no-Takumi arrived in Japan, and erected a miniature mountain with a connecting bridge in the southern garden of the palace in the year 612. This artificial peak seems to have been a symbolic representation of Sumeru, the great mountain located in the middle of the Buddhist universe, which is envisioned as being surrounded by eight oceans and nine subsidiary mountains.

The direct influence of Buddhist ideas on concepts of garden design becomes apparent during the middle of the Heian period. About this time, religious movements whose beliefs centered on salvation in the Buddha Amida's "Pure Land" ('Jôdo') were gradually gaining momentum and strength. According to this philosophy, the "Pure Land" was located in the western reaches of the Buddhist universe, and was composed of beautiful pavilions, overlooking spacious ponds filled perenially with a profusion of lotus blossoms. There, the souls of believers who had invoked the infinite compassion of Amida dwelt in bliss, surrounded by the fragrance of flowers and the sounds of celestial music. The period was market by bisorder and strife, and pessimism and doubt were rampant in all levels of society. Consequently, the new sects who preached that salvation was possible simply through repetition of the simple formula "Namu Amida Butsu" ("Homage to Amida Buddha") gained adherents in great numbers, in court circles as well as among the common populace. In the teachings and art forms of these sects, there is an overall preoccupation with Amida's Paradise. During services, large "Jôdo-mandara" paintings were hung in the worship halls. In them, Amida's Paradise was represented in all its magnificence, with splendid belvederes overhanging lotus-filled ponds. The architectural schemes in these paintings, which represented an idealized arrangement based on Chinese forms, was generally fixed, and with the passing of time, various of the temples of the Jôdo sets gradually came to be built in partial imitation of them, a phenomenon which developed out of the desire to give the parishioners some tangible idea of the beauty and bliss awaiting them in the next world. This development, based on the impulse to give concrete, recognizeable form to an ideal vision of paradise, was important in creating an atmosphere congenial to the religious requirements of the age. At the same time, it gave rise to certain ideas about temple arrangement which are particularly important in the advancement of garden design.

The first manifestations of Jôdo thought in landscape gardening were relatively simple, and may be seen in the installation of a broad lotus pond in front of the main, centrally situated buildings of a complex. The layout of such temple compounds gained complexity with the passing of time, however, and the structures became more elaborate in their execution and design. The best example of these developments is the Hôô-dô ("Phoenix Hall") of the Byôdô-in temple in Uji, the finest surviving structure of the Heian period, which is a close reproduction of Jôdo-mandara icon-paintings, not only in regard to arrangement, but also in its evocation of the sublime atmosphere of the glories of the "Western Paradise".

Thus, the ideal schematic prototypes for such temple complexes existed in paintings, and these were utilized in the actual arrangement of Jôdo temples and other structures influenced by Jôdo thought. "Seven-treasure" ponds, filled with a sea of lotus blossoms, were laid out in conjunction with the main temple buildings, and bridges, of the sort used by the blessed souls when they passed over into paradise, were erected, connecting various parts of the garden.

The arrangement of the garden of the Shômyô-ji in Yokohama, laid out during the latter half of the Kamakura period, shows the strong influence of Jôdo ideas. Its plan is a symbolic representation of the passage from the present world across to a "Pure Land" Paradise. A large part of the garden grounds are covered by a spacious pond, with a single island in its center.

After entering the compound through the Nandaimon ('Great South Gate'), one crosses over an arched bridge to the island and finally along a level bridge to the far shore, where the main temple structure stands. It is of particular interest that these five elements are all situated along a straight axial line. This distinctive garden plan represents one of the clearest examples of the influence of religious ideas on garden composition to be seen in Japan, for it is an attempt at literal interpretation of the paradise scenes common in Jôdo-mandara paintings, transformed into terms of actual garden design.

The influence of Jôdo thought on garden composition varied with time and location; the presence of a few lotus flowers in a modest pond sufficed in some cases, while extensive efforts to realize an accurate equivalent of the schematized ideals seen in paintings occurred in examples such as the Shômyô-ji, just mentioned. The range of variation is ample evidence of the impact and breadth of this influence over the centuries, however, and it is of the greatest importance, not only in the history of temple gardens, but in the development of gardens for private residences as well.

Jôdo ideas are also apparent in the composition of Yoshimitsu's Kitayama-dono garden, where the main structure, the 'Shariden' ('Reliquary Hall', also known as the Kinkaku, or "Golden Pavilion") (P.10) is situated in the center of the arrangement, beside a broad lotus lake containing a rock formation symbolizing the nine mountains and eight seas surrounding Mt. Sumeru, central peak of the Buddhist universe. Furthermore, inspiration for the lake seems to have come from representations of the "Seven Treasure Ponds" usually present in Jôdo paradise paintings.

This influence is equally clear in Yoshimasa's Higashiyama-dono (or Ginkaku, "Silver Pavilion") garden (p. 14), where the main structure looks out across a lotus pond; and the images enshrined in the adjoining Tôgû-dô are appropriately, Amida Buddha and his attendant Bodhisattvas, Kannon and Seishi. Moreover, the name of the Tôgû-dô itself expresses the appeal for rebirth in the Pure Land of Amida's Paradise in the west.

Jôdo thought continued to exert a powerful influence on garden design as late as the Edo period, and it also constitutes an important element in the abstract composition of Zen gardens.

Although the first, early attempts at propagating the concepts of Zen in Japan met with failure, the sect finally took root under the diligent leadership of the priests Eisai (1141–1215) and Dôgen (1200–1253), who traveled to China to study its tenets, and set up monasteries on their return. The successful introduction of the Zen sect took place at a time when the power of the nobility had waned noticeably, and control of the country had largely passed into the hands of the rising military class. Zen ideas struck a responsive chord among the brusk, often unlettered warriors of the period, for its general disregard for intellectual or philosophical approaches to religion, reliance on individual discipline and inner mastery, and emphasis on silent meditation as a means for seeking enlightenment dovetailed well with their own emotional and religious sentiments. Thus, Zen became the main religion of the soldiers who administered the country during the Kamakura period, and they responded generously by erecting a number of great temples for its propagation. During the Muromachi period, its power and influence continued to grow, and it exercised considerable affect on the development of the arts, for the aesthetic canons which grew from its ideas were admired by the military class, at whose hands they became widely diffused.

Zen ideas often seem paradoxical to the outsider, and are not easily explained, but some indication of its approach toward religious questions may be gained from statements such as "To see into one's nature and realize Buddhahood", or "Direct pointing at the heart of man", ideas which stress the importance of penetrating through the exterior surface of things, and seeing straight into their spiritual essence or core. It was inevitable that such a preoccupation would give rise to distinctive art forms.

Among the rare art works in the possession of the Daitoku-ji temple are a set of three paintings executed by the great Chinese Sung dynasty master, Mu Ch'i, which express Zen sentiments in a very interesting manner. The center painting shows the Bodhisattva Kannon. The two flanking works, however, in contrast to the standard practice in such Buddhist paintings, where other deities (such as the Bodhisattvas Monju or Fugen) are usually depicted, consist simply of representations of a monkey and a crane. These serve as symbols of universal truths, and function as a kind of spontaneous, visual sermon. In similar manner, such apparently blasphemous ideas as likening the body of the Buddha to a wooden clog, or comparing his profound teachings to the sound of the babbling of a brook, express the basic Zen objective of penetrating to the heart of things, irrespective of the dictates of conventional religious precedent or custom, and capturing the truth which lies hidden there. Thus, the monkey and crane, sequestered in some pleasant corner deep in the mountains away from the artificial pretentious world of men, live a spontaneous, natural existence, devoid of anxiety, expressing their basic, essential temperaments. The central work showing Kannon also symbolizes Zen ideas, for the deity is not only filled with compassion for mankind, but also entirely free from bias or conceit.

During Muromachi times, Zen thought had a profound effect on the course of Japanese cultural development, and it exercised a unique influence on the progress of garden design, where ideas of abstract composition based on the Zen concept of 'Mu' ("Nothingness") came into vogue. These were intended as a symbolic expression of the attainment of 'Satori', the state of enlightenment which constitutes the ultimate ideal in Zen.

In this development, the broad "natural" gardens of Heian times, with their rich profusion of trees, ponds, shrubs, and running water, were repudiated. Their lavish atmosphere of surrounding nature was rejected in favor of new ideas of sparencess and understatement; and a neoteric concept of beauty, inspired by the transcendental concept of "Nothingness" made its appearance. A distinct tendency toward diminution in scale, and restraint in the use of materials developed, along with a growing inclination to represent nature in a symbolic fashion.

In Muromachi society, especially those levels under the influence of, or in contact with, currents of Zen thought, the attitude toward the function of gardens underwent a marked change. Where gardens had formerly served simply as a location where the spectator viewed the beauties of nature for his casual enjoyment, they now became places where one also meditated, and trained his mind and spirit. Consequently, it is not surprising that certain of the stones used in such enclosures came to be regarded as symbolic of the presence of various of the Buddhist deities. Thus "Three-deity stone-groups" ('sanzon-ishigumi') became common features in certain types of gardens from the Muromachi period on. Composed of a large central boulder, flanked by two smaller ones, these groups were intended to represent typical seated Buddhist triads, such as the Buddha Sakyamuni and his attendants, the Bodhisattvas Manjusri and Samantabhadra. In addition, larger arrangements, meant to represent the Sixteen Arhats, disciples of the historical Buddha, were also set up, utilizing natural boulders of appropriate shapes. A branch temple of the great Zen monastery Daitoku-ji, the Shûon-an ("Ikkyû-ji") located in the southeast suburbs of Kyoto, contains a fine composition of this sort in the garden east of its hôjô (p. 77). The far corner of the garden of the Daitoku-ji Honbô also has a renowned 'sanzon-ishigumi' arrangement which serves additionally as a symbolic waterfall in the garden's composition (p.44). A further variation may be seen in the shoin garden of the Daisen-in, where the vertical 'waterfall' boulder is referred to as the "Kannon-ishi", after the Bodhisattva Kannon, and various of the remaining rocks are likened to other deities, such as Fudô Myôô, Daruma, and various of the Buddha's disciples (p.18).

In Zen thought, art forms are inspired by an idealistic, non-literal orientation toward the expression of religious ideas, and there are few instances of works which might properly be called "iconographical" in the narrow sense of the term. Thus, "paradise" scenes of the sort common in Jôdo art are not to be seen in Zen temples. Rather, paintings such as the Mu Ch'i monkey and crane works, or monochrome landscapes, rendered in a spare, dry manner, which constitute a kind of symbolic vehicle for the expression of abstract, metaphysical concepts are characteristic. In the case of garden design, the medium for communicating these concepts is a unique form of composition known as 'karesansui' (or 'karasenzui', "dry-landscape"), in which living nature is re-organized, abstracted, and condensed. In 1466, the poet-priest Shinzui visited a garden of this type designed by Zeami, and wrote "The distant peaks and rushing streams nearby were altogether marvelous – so absorbing, indeed, that I suddenly lost all thought of returning home!". The garden which impressed him so was very modest in size, and constructed mainly of rocks and gravel. A similar remark about a karesansui garden may be seen in a diary written by the Zen priest Tessen Sôki: "A distance of thirty-thousand leagues – condensed into a few feet and inches!". Thus, one of the chief features of such gardens is the ability to evoke a sense of great distance, a sense of metaphysical space, in the mind of the viewer.

One of the finest examples of a work of this kind is situated adjacent to the shoin of the Daisen-in (p.18). Laid out when the temple was first established in 1509 by the priest Sokan, it is unique in the abstract, conceptualized manner of its composition, which embodies the ideals of Zen thought very succinctly, and it is difficult to imagine that anyone but a Zen monk who had achieved enlightenment could have conceived it. The total composition is achieved in a few dozen square yards, and its main elements consist of a series of skillfully integrated rocks of varying sizes. Two large boulders in the northeast corner evoke the idea of a waterfall, and a low, vertical rock slab in front suffices as a symbolic bridge. A vivid sense of running water is created through the use of passages of white gravel, whose currents, alternately turbulent and then provocatively calm, flow south, to the right. The overall atmosphere is admirably suited for contemplation; soon the viewer is absorbed in the cogent drama before him, his mind filled with a sense of abstract space which defies finite boundaries, like a Sung dynasty monochrome painting.

Another superb example may be seen in the "dry-landscape" garden of the Daitoku-ji Honbô, which covers a larger area, but has certain features in common with the Daisen-in garden. Laid out on a flat, even surface covered with carefully raked gravel, the focal center of the composition is the grouping of shrubs and boulders in the southeast extremity of the enclosure (p. 42). The two largest boulders constitute the symbolic central waterfall while certain of the smaller rocks to each side represent lesser falls and variations in the flow of water. The entire composition is achieved with a lack of detail and direct simplicity which is dramatic in its visual impact, and reveals the Zen conception of "Nothingness" in an impressive manner.

The celebrated "rock garden" of the Ryôan-ji, situated at the foot of Mt. Kinugasa, represents an even more advanced stage of abstract conception (p. 26). Laid out in a flat, rectangular enclosure in front of the hôjô and flanked to the rear by a low earthen wall, the entire composition consists of only fifteen rocks, of dissimilar shape, arranged in intermittent groups which seem to float on the sea of raked gravel. Small patches of moss may be discerned close to some of the rocks, but not a single shrub is to be seen anywhere in the arrangement. There is no sign of discord anywhere and one is struck by the unique beauty of the atmosphere—a kind of taut, silent quality achieved through understatement and simplicity. The basic philosophical point of departure in this work is obviously akin to those which inspired the Daisen-in and Daitoku-ji Honbô gardens just described. Nevertheless, the Ryôan-ji example clearly represents an even greater departure from conventional ideas of garden design, for there is not even a pretense of a symbolic mountain, waterfall or flowing stream. It represents a step beyond, a more congenial accord with concepts of the pure abstract, a symbolic expression of the enlightenment to be gained from meditation.

THE TEA CEREMONY AND GARDENS

The priest Eisai (1141–1215), an important figure in the early propagation of the Zen sect, is generally credited with the introduction of tea cultivation to Japan, following his return from study in China in 1191. He is said to have brought tea seeds back with him, which were planted and raised successfully in the garden of the Kôzan-ji by the monk Myôe. Tea was admired initially for its medicinal properties, and Eisai wrote a treatise (the *Kissayôjôki*) in which he described its value for curative and hygienic purposes. In subsequent years it came into fashion among Zen adepts, for its qualities as a stimulant helped them in the maintenance of mental discipline during their long hours of meditation; and the rites and social forms which evolved from this practice became inherent aspects of Zen behavior and thought.

In Chinese Zen monasteries, the ritual of receiving visitors was usually accompanied by an offering of tea, and the beverage was also drunk by the priests on special occasions. During the Kamakura and Ashikaga periods, many Chinese Zen monks came to Japan to spread the tenets of their faith, and they brought these customs with them. Ikkyû (1394–1481), a noted priest of the Daitoku-ji, is said to have instructed his student Shukô (1423–1502) in certain of these practices, and it was at Shukô's hands that they were first organized into a formal ceremony, and acquired new significance as a form of spiritual training. The Shogun Yoshimasa, builder of the superb "Gin-kaku" pavilion at the foot of Higashiyama, is remembered as a patron of the arts and connoisseur who gathered a coterie of noted playwrights, artists, actors and men of refinement around him, and inspired an impressive outburst of creative activity through his encouragement of their efforts. Yoshimasa was instructed in the Tea Ceremony by Shukô, who also served as a kind of advisor on aesthetic matters to the shogun, and the artistic ideals of the period, which are characterized by a sense of elegant restraint and graceful simplicity, seem to have been influenced significantly by the canons of the Tea Ceremony. One of the foremost masters in the history of the cult is Sen no Rikyû (1520–1591), who not only regulated and codified the ceremony, but also established the basic principles of ritual and deportment ("Sadô, the Way of Tea") which are followed to the present day. Rikyû was a man of many talents–a practitioner of Zen, expert on flower arrangement, and arbiter of taste, whose opinions on aesthetic questions were valued and eagerly sought by various of the great men of the sixteenth century, notably the Taikô, Toyotomi Hideyoshi.

The practice of drinking powdered tea first gained favor among the cultured upper classes of society and members of the Buddhist clergy, who appreciated its refreshing, stimulating qualities; the custom was subsequently spread throughout Japan by priests, and became widely used in temples and monasteries, where its exhilirating affects proved to be of assistance during meditation, when deep concentration was required. As a result of this practice, certain rites and procedures were developed for the drinking of tea, and these gained a spiritual significance with the passing of time. Because of the emphasis placed on meditation in the Zen sect, it is not surprising that the practice of drinking powdered tea became closely associated with the religious ideals and procedures of that branch of Buddhism and that many tea masters have been Zen monks.

Four elements are traditionally regarded to be essential in conducting a Tea Ceremony, and these reveal the spiritual content of "Cha-no-Yu" (the "Tea Ceremony") very clearly.

a) Wa: a concept of pervasive harmony between man, nature and the universe. It expresses the sense of sincerity and congenial intercourse which are motivating ideals in 'Sadô'.

b) Kei: the feelings of mutual veneration and respect that are necessary in human relations, and the concept of personal humility toward all things.

c) Sei: the elements of cleanliness and order that should be present in our surroundings, our thoughts, and in our dealings with others.

d) Jaku: the principle of cultivating a calm mind in a serene, reposeful environment–an indispensible requisite in achieving the main objectives of Sadô–a discerning mind and spiritual awareness.

The first gardens designed to harmonize with the ideals of Cha-no-yu and perform an integral role in its ritual seem to have been laid out during the Momoyama period, when Rikyû was active in establishing the canons and aesthetic forms which have remained of central importance in the history of the Tea Ceremony to the present day. The custom of installing rustic stone lanterns and stone basins in such gardens seems to have developed about this time. In the beginning, these elements were entirely functional, for the lanterns were necessary for illumination during evening functions, and the guests used the water in the stone basins to wash dust from their hands and faces. With the passing of time, however, they assumed a symbolic importance, and became consciously utilized in the composition of the gardens. Tea Ceremony gardens are known as 'roji', and are generally composed along a path leading to the 'chashitsu' ("tea house"), and in the surrounding area in such a manner that the guest feels that he has disassociated himself from the outer world once he has entered and proceeded along the path. In arranging such gardens, the primary objective is to create an atmosphere which is conducive to the serene state of mind necessary for full appreciation of the ceremony.

HOIKUSHA COLOR BOOKS

ENGLISH EDITIONS

Book Size 4″×6″

COLORED ILLUSTRATIONS FOR NATURALISTS

Text in Japanese, with index in Latin or English.

First Issues (Book Size 6″ × 8″)

＜ENGLISH EDITIONS＞

SHELLS
OF
THE
WESTERN
PACIFIC
IN
COLOR

Book Size 7″×10″

〈vol. I〉 by Tetsuaki Kira
(304 pages, 72 in color)
〈vol. II〉 by Tadashige Habe
(304 pages, 66 in color)

FISHES
OF
JAPAN
IN
COLOR

Book Size 7″×10″

by Toshiji Kamohara
(210 pages, 64 in color)